Temperature

BLACKBIRCH PRESS

An imprint of Thomson Gale, a part of The Thomson Corporation

THOMSON

GALE

Detroit • New York • San Francisco • San Diego • New Haven, Conn. • Waterville, Maine • London • Munich

THOMSON

GALE ™

Consultant: Kimi Hosoume
Associate Director of GEMS (Great
  Explorations in Math and Science),
Director of PEACHES (Primary
  Explorations for Adults, Children,
  and Educators in Science),
Lawrence Hall of Science,
University of California,
Berkeley, California

For The Brown Reference Group plc
Text: Chris Woodford
Project Editor: Lesley Campbell-Wright
Designer: Lynne Ross
Picture Researcher: Susy Forbes
Illustrator: Darren Awuah
Managing Editor: Bridget Giles
Children's Publisher: Anne O'Daly
Production Director: Alastair Gourlay
Editorial Director: Lindsey Lowe

For more information, contact
Blackbirch Press
27500 Drake Rd.
Farmington Hills, MI 48331-3535
Or you can visit our Internet site at http://www.gale.com

PHOTOGRAPHIC CREDITS
Ardea: 22; **ARS:** Jack Dykinga 24; **The Brown Reference Group plc:** Edward Allwright 8, 28,
29t, Martin Norris 1, 10b; **Corbis:** Darrell Gulin 27b, David Lees 16, Gabe Palmer 15b; **Hemera:**
5, 9r; **Imagestate:** 9l; **NASA:** 2tr, 10t, 18; **Photodisc:** 6; **Photolibrary.com:** Lori Adamski-Peek 4,
Jan Marcie Bronstein 26, Martyn Chilmaid 13, Michael Leach 23t; **Photos.com:** 2br, 10cl&cr,
14, 19, 20, 21, 27t; **Rex Features:** Henryk T. Kaiser 12; **Robert Harding World Imagery:** 11;
Science & Society: Science Museum 17r; **Science Photo Library:** Paul Whitehill 29b; **Still
Pictures:** Chlaus Lotscher 7, Michael Sewell 25; **Topham:** Science Museum/HIP 17tl&b.

Front cover: **The Brown Reference Group plc:** Edward Allwright

LIBRARY OF CONGRESS CATALOGING-IN-PUBLICATION DATA

Woodford, Chris.
  Temperature / by Chris Woodford.
    p. cm. — (How do we measure?)
  Includes bibliographical references and index.
  ISBN 1-4103-0369-1 (lib. bdg. : alk. paper) — ISBN 1-4103-0525-2 (pbk. : alk.
paper)
  1. Temperature — Juvenile literature. I. Title II. Series: Woodford, Chris. How
do we measure?

  QC271.4.W66 2005
  536'.5--dc22

                                        2004020295

Printed and bound in Thailand
10 9 8 7 6 5 4 3 2 1

Contents

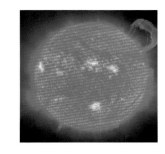

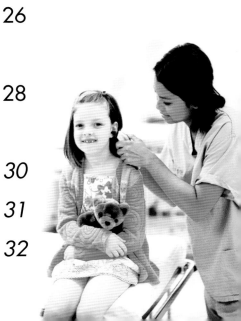

What is temperature?

A summer's day can feel really hot. A winter's day feels much cooler. We can tell the difference between the two using temperature.

Temperature is a measurement of how hot or cold something is.

Temperature and heat

Heat and temperature are not the same. Heat is a kind of energy that things can have. When a metal bar is heated in a fire, it gains a lot of heat energy. Heat energy makes the bar hot. The bar has a high temperature because it is hot. When it is cold the bar has a low temperature.

Sometimes during winter, the temperature is so low that snow falls. People wear lots of thick clothes to keep warm.

On a hot day, the temperature is high. On a cold day, the temperature is lower.

Using thermometers

One way to measure temperature is using a thermometer. A thermometer is like a ruler that measures how hot or cold something is. It has a scale on its side that tells us the temperature. There are many different kinds of thermometers.

Thermometers come in all shapes and sizes. Some are long and thin like rulers, and some are round. They all have a scale that shows temperature.

There are lots of other ways to measure temperature, too.

Measuring temperature can be very useful. It tells us how hot a stove needs to be to cook our dinner. It helps us know if we are sick or healthy. And measuring temperature lets us know if we need to pack warm clothes when we go on vacation.

Figuring out temperatures

Length is easy to measure. We can put a ruler next to a pencil and measure how long it is. But we cannot see temperature. So how can we measure it?

When things get hotter or colder, they change size. If we heat a metal bar in a fire, the bar gets a tiny bit longer. If we cool the bar, it gets shorter.

If we could measure how long the bar was when it was hot and cold, then the length of the bar could tell us something about its temperature.

Water, ice, and steam

Water can help us measure temperature. When it is very cold, water is frozen as solid ice. At everyday temperatures, water is a liquid. When water is very hot, it becomes a gas called steam. If we put a metal bar in a glass of water and the water freezes, the bar must be very cold. If the water boils, the bar must be very hot.

When temperatures are very low, drips of water freeze to form long rods of ice, called icicles.

When it is very hot and sunny (left), water disappears from the soil, which shrinks. Cracks appear in the ground.

Heat changes things

We cannot see temperature, but we can see how heat changes things. We can see how heat makes a metal bar grow longer or how it makes an ice cube melt. We can also see how heat dries the earth and makes it crack.

We can see and measure these changes. That is how we can measure temperature, even though we cannot see it.

Measuring temperature

We can measure temperature with a thermometer. A thermometer is a hollow tube made of glass. Inside the tube is a metal called mercury. The mercury looks like a thin silver line inside the glass.

Like water, mercury is a liquid at ordinary temperatures.

A thermometer is usually like a ruler. It has a scale marked on the outside of the glass. Instead of measuring length, this scale measures how hot or cold something is.

These girls are using a thermometer to measure the temperature of the room they are in.

How do thermometers work?

Mercury in a thermometer is just like a metal bar. When mercury heats up, it gets a little bit longer. When mercury cools down, it gets a little bit shorter.

So mercury moves up and down inside the glass tube as the temperature changes. Mercury moves along the scale, just like a finger moving along a ruler. We can find out the temperature by seeing where the mercury line is on the scale.

When mercury moves down the scale, we know the temperature around us is lower than when it moves higher up the scale.

This picture shows what mercury looks like when it is not in a thermometer. You should never touch mercury because it is poisonous.

Mercury measures

Mercury is a very special metal. At everyday temperatures, it is a liquid. Liquid mercury rises up and down inside a thermometer. Even a small temperature change makes the mercury move quite a lot. Most of the mercury is stored in a bulb at the bottom of the thermometer.

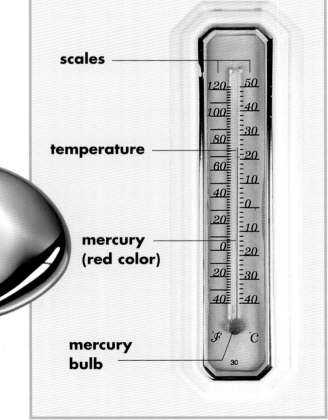

scales

temperature

mercury (red color)

mercury bulb

Temperature scales

Rulers have a scale on them marked in inches or centimeters. Thermometers also have scales on them. Instead of inches, thermometers are marked in units called degrees. A degree is one unit of temperature. A high temperature could be hundreds or thousands of degrees. A low temperature might be just a few degrees.

The Fahrenheit scale

Thermometers can have different scales. The most common scale in the United States is called Fahrenheit. On the Fahrenheit scale, boiling water has a temperature of 212 degrees. That can be written 212°. We call this 212 degrees Fahrenheit, or 212°F. The "F" shows that we are using the Fahrenheit scale.

Freezing water, or ice, has a much lower temperature than

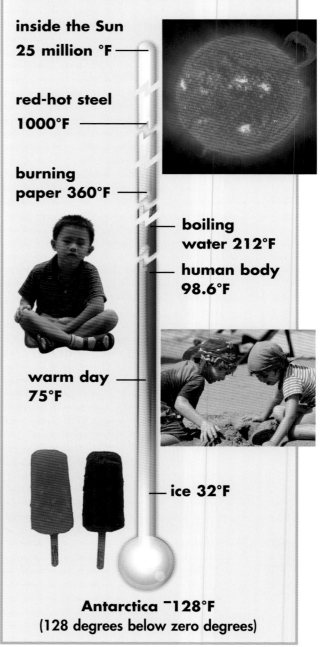

How hot is that?

inside the Sun
25 million °F

red-hot steel
1000°F

burning
paper 360°F

boiling
water 212°F

human body
98.6°F

warm day
75°F

ice 32°F

Antarctica ⁻128°F
(128 degrees below zero degrees)

boiling water. The temperature of ice is 32 degrees Fahrenheit, or 32°F.

Temperatures lower than zero are extremely cold. The coldest temperatures on Earth are on Antarctica. Antarctica is the huge continent, or mass of land, around the South Pole. The lowest temperature ever recorded there was ⁻128°F. This is read as minus 128 degrees Fahrenheit. That temperature is so cold that hardly anything lives in Antarctica.

This digital thermometer shows the temperature as numbers, or digits. Minus 14 degrees Fahrenheit, or ⁻14°F, is very cold indeed.

The centigrade scale

Rulers can be marked in feet and inches. They can also be marked in metric units, such as meters and centimeters. There is also a metric scale of temperature. It is called the centigrade, or Celsius, scale. It is much simpler and easier to use than the Fahrenheit scale. On the centigrade scale, freezing water has a temperature of 0 degrees. Just like a Fahrenheit temperature, this temperature

This thermometer shows that water freezes to form ice at 0°C (or 32°F).

Changing temperatures

If you know a temperature in Fahrenheit, you can also figure out what it would be in centigrade or Celsius. First, subtract, or take away, 32 from the Fahrenheit temperature.

212°F – 32 = 180

Then multiply the result by 5.

180 x 5 = 900

Next, divide that result by 9.

900 ÷ 9 = 100°C

So 212°F is the same as 100°C.

To change centigrade or Celsius into Fahrenheit, first multiply the centigrade temperature by 9.

100°C x 9 = 900

Then divide the result by 5.

900 ÷ 5 = 180

Finally, add 32.

180 + 32 = 212°F

So 100°C is the same as 212°F. If you know a temperature in centigrade or Celsius, it is easy to figure out what it is in Fahrenheit.

can be written as 0°. We say water freezes at zero degrees centigrade, or 0°C. The "C" is a quick way of writing *centigrade*.

Boiling water has a temperature of 100 degrees on the centigrade scale. That can also be written as 100°. We say water boils at one hundred degrees centigrade, or 100°C. Celsius is just another way of saying centigrade. So 100 degrees Celsius is the same as 100 degrees centigrade.

Water boils at a temperature of 100°C (or 212°F).

More thermometers

Ordinary thermometers are sometimes called mercury thermometers. There are several different kinds of thermometers. Medical thermometers are used to measure people's body temperatures. Our body temperature does not usually change very much. That is why medical thermometers have a scale that goes from only 90°F to 108°F. A smaller scale makes them easier to read and more exact.

This nurse is using a digital thermometer placed in a girl's ear.

Maximum and minimum thermometers

Maximum and minimum thermometers are used to study the weather. These thermometers have two tubes of mercury side by side. On any day, one side measures the highest temperature reached, and the other the lowest temperature.

Digital thermometers

Not all thermometers have mercury inside them. Some thermometers measure temperature in different ways.

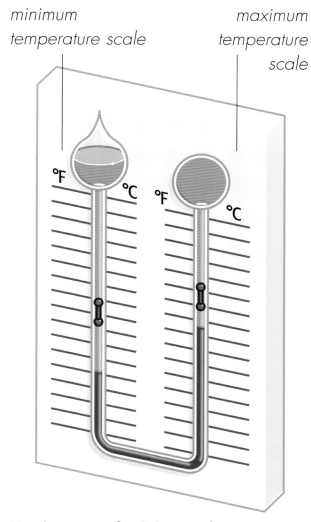

minimum temperature scale

maximum temperature scale

°F °C °F °C

Maximum and minimum thermometers have two scales. One records the hottest temperature, and the other, the lowest temperature.

Digital thermometers measure temperature using electronics. Instead of a scale, they have a digital readout. That shows the exact temperature as a number, like on a digital watch.

Thermostats

Electric heaters have built-in thermometers called thermostats. Thermostats, like the one below, measure the temperature in the room around them all the time. If the temperature gets too hot, the thermostat switches off the heater. When the temperature falls too low, the thermostat switches on the heater again. The thermostat keeps the room temperature at a steady level. Air conditioning units also have thermostats in them. They switch on a fan when the temperature is too hot. When the temperature is too cold, they switch off the fan again.

Thermometer inventors

The first thermometer was made in 1592 by a brilliant Italian scientist named Galileo (1564–1642). His thermometer was an upside-down glass jar filled with air and water. Scientists soon found other substances worked much better instead. A German scientist named Daniel Gabriel Fahrenheit (1686–1736) also made a thermometer. In 1714 he discovered that it worked best of all using mercury inside. That is how the modern

Galileo's thermoscope

Galileo's early thermometer was called a thermoscope. He took a rounded jar with a very long glass neck and warmed it up. Then he turned the jar upside down and dipped its neck into a bowl of water. As the air in the jar cooled, it shrank a little. That pulled some of the water up the glass neck. So Galileo had made a simple thermometer a bit like the mercury ones we still use.

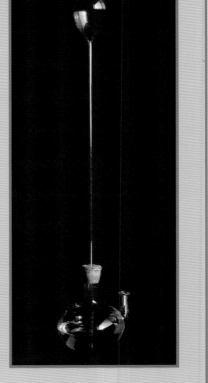

A model of Galileo's thermoscope, which used water rather than mercury to measure temperature.

Swedish scientist Anders Celsius invented the temperature scale now called the centigrade or Celsius scale.

mercury thermometer was invented. Ten years later, Fahrenheit figured out the temperature scale that is now named for him.

In 1742 Swedish scientist Anders Celsius (1701–1744) invented the other popular temperature scale, called the centigrade scale. The "centi" part of the word *centigrade* means 100. There are 100 degrees between the freezing point of water, 0°C, and the boiling point of water, 100°C.

Some people call this scale the Celsius scale after Anders Celsius.

This thermometer is based on Galileo's original thermoscope. It has multicolored glass bubbles floating in a column of water. The lowest bubble tells us what the temperature is.

Absolute temperature

Everyday substances like water are made of tiny invisible particles. These particles are called atoms. Groups of atoms are called molecules.

When something is hot, its molecules move around. The hotter something is, the faster its molecules move. The colder it is, the slower its molecules move.

What if we could cool something so much that its molecules stopped moving altogether? We would reach the lowest possible temperature. That temperature is called absolute zero. Absolute zero is ⁻460°F, or ⁻273°C. There is no temperature colder than that.

Scientists use two temperature scales that start

Off the scale?

Absolute zero is the lowest temperature anything could ever reach. But no one really knows what the hottest is. Inside the Sun (right), the temperature is about 25 million °F, or 14 million K. On Earth, scientists have made explosions with temperatures as high as 180 million °F!

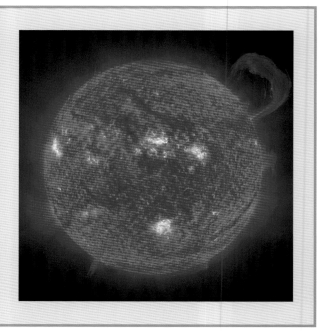

Although this iceberg is icy cold, it is still nowhere near as cold as absolute zero.

off at absolute zero. They are called the Kelvin scale and the Rankine scale. The Kelvin scale measures upward from absolute zero in degrees centigrade. The Rankine scale measures upward from absolute zero in degrees Fahrenheit. On the Kelvin scale, our body temperature is 310 Kelvin (K), water boils at 373 K, and paper burns at 460 K.

Red hot

When fires burn, they are often yellow or red. Lots of things change color when they heat up. If we heat an iron bar in a fire or in a very hot oven called a furnace, the iron bar slowly changes color. First it becomes a dull red-brown. As the iron bar gets hotter, it glows red, orange, yellow, and finally white. When a metal bar is so hot that it turns red, we say it is red hot. Its temperature is about 1750°F. A yellow-hot bar is about 2000°F.

Molten metal in a furnace glows orange and yellow. A furnace is a very hot oven that heats iron. The steelworker wears a protective suit because of the heat.

This metal bolt (above) is so hot that it glows red. We often say hot things are red hot.

Color changes

Color changes can help us measure temperature. Blacksmiths know they can shape metal only when it is very hot. They heat it until it glows orange-red. Then they know it is hot enough to bend and hammer into shape.

Heat and light

Hot things give out heat. We can feel the heat from a fire, for example. Some hot things also give out light. Most light bulbs work by heating a thin piece of wire inside them. The wire gets very hot and gives out heat and light energy. When hot things give out light, we know they are very hot indeed.

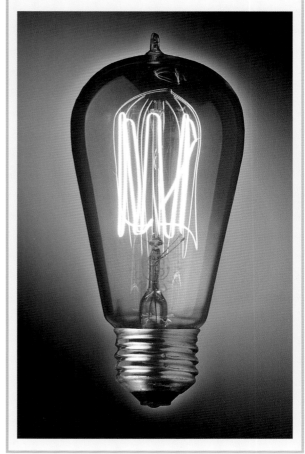

Temperature in action

People measure temperature for many reasons. Measuring temperature is very helpful in factories. Many things, such as plastics, are best made at certain temperatures. Fresh food is also best stored at low temperatures. That helps stop the food from going bad.

We can save energy and protect our surroundings making houses that hold in heat. To do this, we take photographs of houses using thermal cameras. Thermal cameras see heat instead of light. They show the parts of a house where most heat

Cricket thermometer

A cricket is a kind of thermometer. Crickets chirp more often when it is hotter and less often when it is colder. Listen for a cricket and count how many times it chirps in 15 seconds. Add 40 to that number. The answer you get is the temperature in degrees Fahrenheit!

escapes, such as the windows and the roof. We can then insulate those areas by covering them with special materials to keep our homes warmer.

Body heat
Temperature also lets us see in the dark. Thermal pictures, or images, help rescue teams find people who get lost at

Some animals, such as this slender loris, come out at night. They can be seen by using thermal cameras.

night. A person's body gives off heat. So we can see a person's body with a thermal camera even when it is dark. We can also use thermal cameras to see animals that come out at night.

Measuring the weather

One important reason for measuring temperature is so we can forecast the weather. Earth's weather is caused mostly by the Sun. When the Sun shines, it sends heat energy to Earth. That makes Earth warm up.

During the year, different parts of our planet have more hours of daylight than others. Also, when the Sun is higher in the sky, its

This is an example of a temperature chart. The higher bars mean higher temperatures in those months.

These people are launching a weather balloon to measure the temperature high up in the sky.

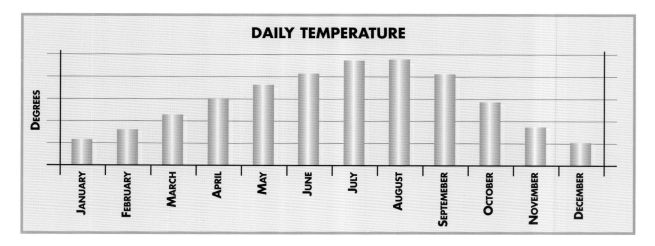

DAILY TEMPERATURE

DEGREES

JANUARY | FEBRUARY | MARCH | APRIL | MAY | JUNE | JULY | AUGUST | SEPTEMBER | OCTOBER | NOVEMBER | DECEMBER

rays are stronger and warmer. So different parts of our planet warm up by different amounts.

That means different parts of Earth have different temperatures. And that is what causes the weather.

Temperature charts

Different places on Earth have different types of weather through the year. Some places are hot and sunny. Others are cold and wet. The type of weather a place has is called its climate. We can see what kind of climate a place has by looking at a chart of its temperature. That shows how temperature changes through the year. The high bars show the warmer months, and the low bars show the cooler months.

Ice cold

The North and South poles are the coldest places on Earth, but hardly anyone lives there. The coldest place where anyone lives is a village called Oymyakon. It is in a part of Russia called Siberia. In 1933 Oymyakon had the lowest temperature ever recorded on Earth. It was −90°F, or −68°C.

These Inuit children live in Alaska. They live in one of the coldest places on Earth, so they wear thick clothes made from animal skin and fur.

Body temperature

Living things can survive only if the temperature is just right for them. Lizards, fish, and many other creatures die if it gets too hot or too cold. If a factory drains hot water into a river, the river warms up. If the river becomes too hot, all the fish in it die.

Cold-blooded animals

Fish, snakes, and lizards are cold-blooded creatures. That does not mean they have cold blood. Cold-blooded animals cannot make their own body heat. To warm up, they have to take heat from around them. So, lizards bask on rocks until they are warm enough to get active. To cool down, they move somewhere less hot.

People and many other animals are warm blooded. Their body temperature stays the same on hot, sunny days as on cold, wintry days. But fish are cold blooded—their temperature depends on the water they swim in.

Sick or healthy?

Doctors take people's temperature to tell if they are sick or healthy. A person's body temperature is normally 98.6°F, or 37°C. If people are sick, their body temperature can climb much higher. In 1980 an American named Willie Jones caught heat stroke on a very hot day. His temperature rose to nearly 116°F, or 47°C—the highest temperature anyone's body has ever reached!

Doctors can tell whether this girl is sick by measuring her temperature. If it is too high, she might be sick.

Warm-blooded animals

Birds, people, and furry animals like cats, dogs, and horses are warm-blooded. Warm-blooded creatures make their own body heat. The food they eat makes heat energy that warms them from the inside.

Feathers or thick fur keeps warm-blooded animals warm in winter. In summer, the fur grows less thick, so the animals keep cool. People wear clothes to keep warm, and we drink cold liquids to help cool us down.

Arctic ground squirrels are the only warm-blooded furry animals that can lower their body temperature to below freezing. That helps them live through freezing arctic winters.

Testing temperature

You will need:

- Several liquid-crystal thermometer strips
- Some things around your home to test
- A pencil and paper

Can you guess which is hottest?

1 Think of five or ten things around your home whose temperature you can test. You might test:
- A sunny window ledge
- Your arm
- A cold faucet
- Different materials, such as paper, metal, or a wall tile.

2 Make a list of these things on a piece of paper.

3

3 Touch each item one at a time. Does each one feel hot or cold? Compare each one to the other objects on your list. Does it feel hotter or colder?

4 Make a list of the objects in order from hottest to coldest. Put what you think is the hottest object at the top and the coldest at the bottom.

Measuring the temperature

5 Now place a liquid-crystal thermometer strip on each object.

6 Wait a few moments for the temperature to settle. Then read the temperature off the strip.

7 Write down the temperature, in degrees Fahrenheit, for each item on your list.

8 Did you figure out correctly which things were the hottest and which were the coldest?

Liquid-crystal thermometers

A liquid-crystal thermometer is a plastic strip containing a special liquid in clear, thin pockets. The pockets have numbers printed on them. As the temperature rises, the liquid in the pockets changes color and brightens. Then the number on the pocket can be seen. That number is the temperature.

Glossary

absolute temperature A temperature measured on a scale that starts at absolute zero.

absolute zero The lowest temperature that can ever be reached.

atom A very small piece of substance.

body temperature The normal temperature of a person, 98.6°F (37°C).

Celsius A temperature scale figured out by Anders Celsius. Also called the centigrade scale.

centigrade A temperature scale based on the temperatures of ice and boiling water. Also called the Celsius scale.

compound A substance made by joining together two or more other substances.

degree A single unit of temperature.

digital thermometer A thermometer that shows the temperature in numbers, like a digital watch.

energy The ability of something to do work (such as pushing of pulling) to make something happen.

Fahrenheit A temperature scale figured out by Daniel Fahrenheit.

heat A type of energy that makes something hot or cold.

Kelvin A temperature scale that starts at absolute zero and measures upward in degrees centigrade.

mercury A metal that is used inside many common thermometers.

molecule A group of joined atoms.

Rankine A temperature scale that starts at absolute zero and measures upward in degrees Fahrenheit.

red hot A temperature so hot that it makes something glow red.

scale A set of equal lines, marked on something like a ruler or thermometer, to help us measure.

temperature A measurement of how hot or cold something is. It is not the same as heat.

thermal Describes something of, or caused by, heat.

thermal image A kind of photograph (taken by a thermal camera) in which hot things show up.

thermometer An instrument for measuring temperature.

thermostat A device that switches heaters and air conditioners on or off to keep a room at the right temperature.

Find out more

Books

Alison Auch, *That's Hot!* Minneapolis, Minnesota: Compass Point, 2002.

Chris Kensler, *Secret Treasures and Magical Measures: Adventures in Measuring: Time, Temperature, Length, Weight, Volume, Angles, Shapes and Money.* New York: Kaplan, 2003.

Darlene Stille and Sheree Boyd, *Temperature: Heating Up and Cooling Down (Amazing Science).* Minneapolis, Minnesota: Picture Window Books, 2004.

Dorling Kindersley, *e-Science Encyclopedia.* New York: Penguin Books, 2004.

Web sites

Graphing the temperature
Make your own temperature-climate graph
www.miamisci.org/hurricane/graphtemp.html

Temperature converter
Converts Fahrenheit to centigrade
www.albireo.ch/temperatureconverter

Yahooligans! Temperature
Some useful sites about the physics of temperature
yahooligans.yahoo.com/Science_and_Nature/Physical_Sciences/Physics/Temperature

Index